T0208338

A LIGHT FROM WITHIN

INSPIRATIONAL POEMS OF A CHILD'S STRUGGLE THROUGH TRAUMA

NIKKI KELLY

authorHOUSE®

AuthorHouse™
1663 Liberty Drive
Bloomington, IN 47403
www.authorhouse.com
Phone: 833-262-8899

Published by AuthorHouse 10/05/2021

ISBN: 978-1-6655-2357-8 (sc)
ISBN: 978-1-6655-2360-8 (hc)
ISBN: 978-1-6655-2361-5 (e)

Library of Congress Control Number: 2021920690

Print information available on the last page.

Any people depicted in stock imagery provided by Getty Images are models, and such images are being used for illustrative purposes only. Certain stock imagery © Getty Images.

This book is printed on acid-free paper.

Contents

Adoption

School

Sexual Assault

PTSD and Miscellaneous Emotions

To Kathy Ryan

For seeing in me what no one else did. For believing in me and teaching me to believe in myself. For showing me the strength I had inside and how to properly direct it. For the countless talks and lessons learned, and for *always* being my "Keeper."

Adoption

If my life was a book, it would have the wrong
cover and start with chapter 2.

Perspectives

Today is so hard for me,
Just having to let you go.
It is the best choice, you see,
Made from love, I hope you know.

A part of me I can't keep.
Loving, missing, mourning you.
Nights, crying myself to sleep,
Questioning "What did I do?"

I love and miss you so.
This time has been a pleasure.
They will tell you so you know.
Now you are theirs to treasure.

*

Today's a great day for me,
Finally bringing you home.
We've waited so long, you see.
Now you're here, we're not alone.

We have tried and tried to conceive.
Depressed, looking for options,
Then it's you we receive.
A precious gift, adoption.

We will love you, hold you tight,
This special gift from above.

We will teach you wrong from right,
Show you how much you are loved.

*

Today's confusing to me.
I don't know where I belong.
One mom full of joy I see.
For the other I still long.

I know I'm young and have no voice.
I can't tell you how I feel.
Please know this was not my choice,
And this pain inside is real.

You need to reassure me,
Show me how much I am loved.
Because I'm an adoptee,
Given to you from above.

Through Adopted Eyes

Hello ... Mommy, where did you go?
Your heartbeat, your smell, they're all I know.
Where are you? Something's wrong.
I just got here; already I don't belong.

Did I do something wrong, are you mad at me?
I'll do better; just wait and see.
Come back; I'll be good and do what you say.
Please don't leave, don't throw me away.

It's been months, and I feel so alone.
Why won't you come back, take me home?
I need you, can't you see?
I'm lost and confused with no identity.

Where are we going?
What is this place?
Who are these people
With smiles on their face?

Oh no, not you too!
You're leaving; what am I supposed to do?
I can't stay here; nothing's the same.
My memories are fading; they changed my name!

You look so happy; it's your special day.
But I feel unwanted and thrown away.
Your pain is over; what a relief.
You'll need to guide me through my grief.

There are so many things you must know
In order for our relationship to grow.
It's not the same; it's different for me.
I wasn't born to you; I'm an adoptee.

Hold me skin to skin.
Let me feel you from within.
You have to do this, you just must.
I need to learn how to trust.

Teach me my history,
How our family came to be.
You bring it up;
Don't just leave it up to me.

Answer my questions.
Please don't be sad
If I shut down and
My anger gets bad.

This is my life
But not my choice.
I was too young.
I had no voice.

A Not so Happy Birthday

The day I was born
No one was excited.
Plans had been made,
Adoption decided.

Quickly whisked away
The moment I was born,
Left in a room, all alone,
Learning how to mourn.

Stuck in a corner,
Still all alone,
In this place called
A "foster home."

Never being held
And always alone.
Learning independence,
How to do things on my own.

Once again
It's time to go.
Where to now
I don't know.

Another New Place
How long will it last?
Will I ever understand
My traumatic past?

This will be
My last stop.
They've decided
To adopt.

I just hope
They're ready for me.
It's so different
Raising an adoptee.

Explanations

Explaining adoption
Is hard, you see.
Perception is different
When you're one of the three.

Birth moms make a choice;
They don't just up and leave.
Adopted parents make a choice
When they find they can't conceive.

Then you have those who think
If you just bring this child home,
Everything will be just fine
If you raise them as your own.

But this child has a past
They really need to know.
Or these feelings deep inside
Become confusing as they grow.

They will have questions,
A natural curiosity.
But be careful with your words
When talking to an adoptee.

People will tell you
No question is dumb.
They weren't adopted
Cuz I've heard a ton.

I was adopted,
Not "given up" or "thrown away."
What a rude and hurtful
Thing to say.

I don't know where she is.
I don't know why she left.
But these *are* my parents.
They're not fake, foster, or step.

I have no answers,
Just questions, you see.
I don't understand,
And it's confusing to me.

I was adopted,
But I'm not an adoptee.
Adoption is only a part of me.
It is *not* my identity.

A Bond That Can't Be Severed

I'm just an infant.
Immediately I'm tore
From my mother.
All alone, I mourn.

I'm so alone.
And I look around,
But my mother
Can't be found.

Months go by
Before I get a home.
It's very nice,
But I feel so alone.

You can't replace her,
I'm sorry to say.
But it's not your fault
I feel this way.

There's a hole in my heart
Only she can fill.
I can't love you
Or hurt her, it will.

I can't tell you how I feel
Even if I knew.
I just want my "real" mom,
And I can tell that isn't you.

I don't mean to hurt you.
I don't mean to push you away.
But inside I am hurting
Every single day.

You think I'm independent.
It's really a lack of trust.
I've already learned if I want it done,
Do it myself I must.

I can't depend on anyone.
Who knows when they will leave?
It doesn't matter if it's true,
It is what I believe.

I will grow up wondering
About this woman I don't know,
And constantly searching
For the mom who let me go.

Not the Same

You say it's the same,
But how can that be?
I wasn't born to you.
I'm an adoptee.

I wasn't placed in her arms
Just after I was born.
I was left all alone,
Learning how to mourn.

I didn't leave the hospital
With whom I had arrived.
I went off to foster care,
Learning to survive.

When I finally got a "forever" home,
Don't tell me that was the same.
Ripped away from all I'd known,
Placed with strangers who changed my name.

It's not the same.
I am different from my peers.
They have already started to bond,
But for me, it could take years.

I've bounced around
From place to place,
Constantly searching
For a familiar face.

I've learned that
Independence is a must,
And that I may never learn
How to trust.

I've learned that
My feelings aren't real,
And this pain inside
Is really no big deal.

I've learned that
I'm ungrateful, and I have bad genes.
But I don't even understand
What any of that means.

You say we're the same,
That I am a part of you.
We look nothing alike,
And you don't enjoy the things I do.

I don't understand,
Don't feel I belong,
And can't be who I am
When you see it as wrong.

You've tried so hard
To erase my past.
I have no memories,
But these feelings last.

I feel and emptiness
Deep inside

Because of these secrets
You make me hide.

I can't talk.
I'm unable to grieve.
I don't understand.
But you don't even believe.

Adoptees are different
From their birth peers.
We protect our a-parents
And hide from them our tears.

Hole in My Heart

There's a hole in my heart
Where "something" used to be.
What it was not "allowed" to know
Because I'm an adoptee.

You tell me about the hole,
And even why it's there,
But tell me nothing else
So that hole I can repair.

You try to fill the hole
With things that don't belong.
You can have my heart,
But this hole you don't belong.

This hole is getting bigger.
It feels like someone died.
You don't understand these feelings,
So I keep them locked inside.

This hole in my heart
Holds a pain you'll never know.
The only ones who understand,
Adoptees and the mothers who let us go.

Something's Missing

I don't understand
These feelings I feel.
All I know
Is my pain is real.

They say I'm too young,
I can't possibly mourn
This woman from whose
Arms I was torn.

It doesn't make sense.
I have no memory,
But my heart is breaking
For the mom I can't see.

My parents are good;
I don't go without.
But my other mom
Is all I think about.

I fantasize about
How great it would be
If she would come
And rescue me.

My life is fine.
I have many friends,
But I feel an emptiness
Deep within.

I don't understand
Why I feel this way.
I just want to see her
In the worst way.

I can't tell you
Just how I feel
When you don't believe
This pain can be real.

They say I'm lucky,
It could be worse.
But you don't understand
How bad this hurts.

I don't dislike
Where I'm at.
But there's a connection
That I lack.

I don't understand,
And I get so annoyed.
But I do know only she
Can fill this void.

Searching to Belong

As I look around,
The people I see,
Hard not to notice
They're nothing like me.

My dark curly hair,
My olive skin tone
No one else shares, and
I feel so alone.

Who do I look like?
Where do I belong?
Are questions I have.
For answers I long.

I live in a house
Where no one's the same.
I know they love me;
They gave me their name.

It's not who I am.
This name is not me.
I'm just so confused.
I'm an adoptee

Missing Pieces

There is a part of me
I just don't understand.
Always curious,
Wondering who I am.

How can I know
Who I will be
With a past
I can't see?

So many questions,
But answers, there are none
About a decision made
Before my life begun.

I feel so empty
Deep inside.
But I can't explain
Exactly why.

I'm confused.
How can it be
I miss a woman
I've never seen?

I feel so guilty
You get so sad.
But I want to know
So, so bad.

I'll stay quiet,
Internalize this pain,
Start believing
I'm to blame.

I'll wonder what I did
That was so very wrong
To have to live a life
Feeling I'll never belong.

Identity Search

Who am I?
Who will I be?
I'm lost, confused,
With no identity.

You changed my name
When I came to you,
Erasing a past
I never knew.

You spoke of adoption
And off to a great start.
But as it got harder,
You seemed to fall apart.

I ask these questions
Because I need to know.
The answers you give
Will help me to grow.

But when I ask,
You just seem sad.
So I shut down,
Start feeling bad.

I'll keep my questions
To myself,
Never asking
For any help.

I will protect you
As I grow,
Hiding my feelings
For a mom I don't know.

But at some point
That will change.
This pain inside
Will turn to rage.

That's not what I want.
I wish you could see
Just how much
This means to me.

Adoption is a part of me,
But it's not who I am.
I want to learn from my past,
So I can understand.

Wondering

I still think about you every day.
I wonder where you are, if you're doing okay.
Do I have a sister, maybe a brother?
And who is this woman that I call mother?

So many things go through my head
Each night as I lie in bed.
Do you miss me, do you grieve?
And why is it you had to leave?

I often wonder if you're reminded of me
With every baby that you see.
So many questions I have, you see.
Something feels missing inside of me.

I can't understand, missing you so,
This woman I may never know.
I don't understand these feelings I feel,
But this pain inside is very real.

Will I ever feel that I belong?
Will I get answers for which I long?
Or is this just life for me,
The price I pay being an adoptee?

Adopted Confusion

Being adopted
Can be rough.
Your questions
Make it twice as tough.

You ask things
I wish I knew.
But I have no answers
To give to you.

All I've been told
Is positive, you see.
Inside, I feel different;
It's confusing to me.

I'm told I'm special.
A gift, they say.
But if that were true,
Why didn't she stay?

I go to school
Day after day.
So tired of hearing,
"You were thrown away."

I wasn't, just
Left on the curb.
My mother loved me.
You're being absurd.

I hear all these things.
What do I believe?
Did she really love me,
Or just up and leave?

When your head and your heart
Can't seem to agree,
You're lost, confused,
With no identity.

And you have more questions
Than answers, you see,
Just what it's like
Growing up an adoptee.

The Adoption Gap

How do I know
Just how I feel,
When all I'm told
Is, "It's not real"?

I have these feelings
I don't understand.
I need to know
Just who I am.

It feels like something is missing.
I can't make it go away.
It's not that I'm ungrateful.
I know that's what you say.

If I wasn't born to you,
Where did I come from?
My history is missing.
Inside I just feel numb.

You can't imagine
What it's like
With an empty gap
In your life.

I don't know where I was
Or what happened to me.
And not one picture
Have I ever seen.

Will I ever understand
These feelings I feel,
And finally know
My pain is real?

Growing Up and Moving On

Who am I to you,
What do you see
Every time
You look at me?

There's more to me
Than you know.
But your main concern
Is your control.

You can't just mold me
A certain way.
I just won't fit;
I'm not made of clay.

You can teach me
To be like you,
But understand
I have a past too.

You've taught me things
To help me grow.
But now it's time
You let me go.

You are my dad;
You were my best friend.
I'm moving on.
It's not the end.

A Book of Confusion

Oh, you're going to
Love this book!
I'll leave it here
For you to look.

What's the matter?
You look confused.
It's OK that
This book is used.

Don't worry
Who had it last!
It's no big deal.
It's in the past.

Who cares
The cover's wrong?
Get over it,
And move along.

Yes, I know
It's missing chapters.
Stop asking questions!
I have no answers!

Just keep reading.
It will be fine.
It should make sense
At some point in time.

For you, this is just a book,
But this is life for me.
My entire life's confusing
Because I'm an adoptee.

The Adoption Puzzle

Family, like a puzzle,
Is beautiful when complete.
They fit together nicely.
With that I can't compete.

I feel like a piece
From another box.
Connections can be made,
But nothing ever locks.

Our ends just butt together,
Or they loosely fit.
Our connections aren't strong;
I'm worried they will quit.

This picture on my face
Is different, you see.
I'm just here to fill a space
That used to be empty.

There's another box
Where I belong,
Or their picture
Will also be wrong.

Like a puzzle piece
That just looks wrong.
Adoptees search forever
To find where they belong.

School

Having a learning disability and being dyslexic is not a curse, you see. It can make my life a bit chaotic, but it also makes me, me."

Mistaken Assumptions

How can you think
This is just a stage,
Blaming adoption
For my frustration and rage?

You don't know
What's going on.
You just assume,
And you are wrong.

You're not asking
The right questions, you see.
This has nothing to do
With being an adoptee.

Oh great.
Another book
About adoption.
I just can't look!

I don't want to read.
It's not for me,
And I'm done talking
About being an adoptee!

You just get mad.
Mom starts to cry.
I'm so confused,
And I don't know why.

What can I do
To avoid all this,
Get sent to my room
So I pitch a fit?

Then for a while
Things calm down.
With no problems seen,
No issues are found.

Third grade
Is not that hard,
But I got an F
On my report card.

I didn't fail
Science, math, or history.
No, it's handwriting
That's an issue for me.

You have me sit
And try to write.
Then that, too,
Becomes a fight.

I can't do this,
Can't you see?
Why won't someone
Just listen to me?

I don't want to sit.
I just want to leave.
What can I do
To make you believe?

So I cover the article
And start to trace,
So I can get you
Off my case.

I continue to practice.
I continue to try.
I don't want anyone else
Asking me why.

Then once again
Things calm down.
Now seventh grade,
And no one's around.

Things at home
Are getting worse.
My entire life's
Just one big curse.

You say I'm not taking
School seriously,
And now everyone's
Giving up on me.

They move me around
From class to class.
They call me lazy
And a pain in the ass.

You think I'm so stupid,
But how can that be?
I've come so far
Not letting anyone see.

I've fooled you.
Yes indeed,
You still don't know
I can barely read.

Unseen Struggles

I don't know why,
And it frustrates me
That school is so much
Harder for me.

I don't understand
What you say.
Why won't you listen,
Explain things a different way?

Something is different,
But I can't explain.
So you blow me off,
Call me a pain.

You get so angry,
Start throwing blame.
I shut down
Because of shame.

I know I'm not stupid,
But I'm not the same.
My friends write stories;
I can't write my own name!

Our books are different,
I have no doubt.
Mine has words
Randomly floating about.

No one will listen.
They say it's a stage.
My frustrations building
And turning to rage.

I don't know what to do.
I can't make you see.
So I'll do my best and hide
What's really wrong with me.

Getting By

It's the same ole thing
Night after night.
Schoolwork always
Becomes a fight.

You get so mad,
Repeating what you say.
But it's not working.
Find a different way.

I don't understand
What you're talking about.
It makes no sense.
Sound *what* out?

You say it's easy
And throw a fit.
It's not for me.
I want to quit!

Fighting like this
Doesn't work for me.
What can I do
So no one can see?

I start to compensate
Just to get by.
So much easier
Out of sight and mind.

Challenges

I'm a typical kid,
Most people would say.
I have many friends
With whom I play.

I love to play ball,
To skate, to ski.
But all of these things
Come easy to me.

When I go to school
My brain goes crazy.
I don't understand,
So they call me lazy.

I've tried to explain
Just what I see,
But no one wants
To listen to me.

Hooked on Phonics,
It's just not me.
Letters making sounds
Is confusing, you see.

I hear what you say,
And I do understand.
But something goes wrong
Between my brain and my hand.

Anytime I try to read
It gets me so frustrated.
I don't understand what's wrong with me;
I just know I hate it.

I can look at a word
Five different times,
And I'll see it
Five different ways.

Bs become Ds,
And sometimes Ps.
And don't get me started
On q's and g's.

I don't understand
What it's all about.
So I'll stay silent
Til I figure it out.

Falling through the Cracks

It's so frustrating to me,
And you get so annoyed.
I can't explain what's "wrong" with me,
So reading I avoid.

You think that you can trick me.
I've seen how hard you've tried.
All you're doing really
Is making it easier to hide.

I've learned many tricks along the way
To make others believe.
I've learned it's not what I say
But how it is perceived.

I've learned to compensate
And not let anyone see.
Struggling in silence,
Thinking something's "wrong" with me.

I was so behind for my age.
How could you not see
What you thought was just a stage
Was really a learning disability?

If They Only Knew

Why am I standing here
Trying to explain
When no one believes me,
So I take the blame?

Proven guilty
Before being tried,
But the truth is
I never lied.

I'm told no one wants me
In their class.
I'm a waste of time
And a pain in the ass.

One last shot;
Next stop is jail.
Don't imagine anyone
Will post my bail.

I've screwed up so bad
At only thirteen.
They tell me that
I'll never amount to anything.

I am still so young,
But my future they can't see.
I'm no longer worth their time,
So they're giving up on me.

Not one adult in my life
Believes I will succeed.
But you just watch; I'll show them.
First … I must learn to read.

If they only knew what was going on,
I wonder what they'd say.
No one knows how hard I struggle
Just to get by day to day.

A Teacher Who Cared

The last thing I remember
Before leaving junior high,
A teacher called me out,
And it wasn't to say, "Goodbye."

I'd never amount to anything
And in prison by eighteen
Is what she had to say to me
When I was just thirteen.

I didn't believe what she said.
I knew it wasn't me.
But I did believe that everyone
Had given up on me.

I felt I had no chance at all.
Seemed pointless to even try.
But I'd be fine; I had a plan
To stay low and just get by.

My first class, my freshman year,
Things began to change.
I had a teacher I actually liked,
But to me it just seemed strange.

I knew she would help me with any class.
But that was her job, to help me to pass.
I could go to her room just to escape.
She'd talk to me, make me feel safe.

As time went on, I grew to respect
This lady, who had such an effect.
Being a teacher, she seemed to love,
Being so willing to go beyond and above.

I could never say just how I feel,
Especially not out loud.
So I live my life every day,
Trying to make her proud.

I am a better student
Because of the knowledge that she shared.
But I am a better person
Because of a teacher who really cared.

School Dazed

I know there's something "wrong" with me.
I don't know what or why.
I can't explain or make you see.
You won't listen when I try.

I see it causing issues;
Everyone's full of stress.
Now I'm even more confused.
Who cares? My writing's a mess.

Just one more thing I must hide
And not let anyone see.
I do my best, I've really tried,
It's just harder for me.

My questions are not stupid.
I'm not playing a game.
I ask to feel included,
Shut down because of shame.

Skipping class to avoid a test,
Afraid I'll never succeed.
Still trying hard to do my best
To hide that I can't read.

It's getting harder for me.
I still don't understand why
I can't fix what's wrong with me.
Believe me, I have tried!

When I look down and start to read,
I see the same as you.
As I move on and pick up speed,
The crazy things they do.

Words become distorted, you see,
With letters floating in space,
Making it confusing to me
And hard to keep my place.

My secret is out; I can finally see
Why things have been so hard for me.
I have a learning disability.
There is *nothing* "wrong" with me.

Dyslexia

I am dyslexic.

I have a reading disability.
There is nothing wrong with me.
I see the world differently.

I am very creative,
With a great imagination.
I see a different perspective.

I have strengths and weaknesses too.
I am not slow; I have a high IQ.
I learn different than you.

Not everything comes easily.
Reading and comprehension are harder for me.
I have a learning disability.

I am not stupid.
(Now read it again, from the bottom up.)

Dyslexic Pride

When I grow up,
What will I be?
Anything I want.
Wait and see.

I am
Just like you,
With hopes, dreams,
And many goals too.

But I see the world
From a different view.
Learning is different
For me than you.

You'd never know,
Once I'm done,
The struggles I had
Before I'd begun.

The end result
Is the same, you see.
But I arrived here
Differently.

I am who I am.
I'll be who I'll be,
Doing it with pride
And a learning disability.

A Look into Me

Please take my hand.
Let me help you to understand.
Slip on my shoes, and walk with me.
Let me show you what it's like to be me

The minute I wake, my head's a mess.
Do I eat first, or do I get dressed?
Running around, looking for clothes,
We're going to be late again, I suppose.

I get in trouble for, "bouncing around."
But I can't focus; my head's on the playground.
I do pay attention when you speak.
But I open my book, and it all looks Greek.

There's so much in my head I can't organize.
My desk's a mess; I can't find my supplies.
It's hard for me, and I struggle to get by.
But no one seems to notice just how hard I try.

My insides get jittery; I can't hold it in.
I talk a mile a minute, say all my friends.
I can't just walk; it's much too slow.
I'm so full of energy—I just go, go, go.

I arrive home, but of course I forgot
My homework assignment and my lunch box.
Then each night I have a routine,
Checking the locks, making sure my floor is clean.

Jump into, bed and my mind still races—
Things I can do; I just want to go places.
Being me is crazy no doubt.
I just go and go, and then ... lights out!

A Challenging Path to Success

I don't see
An exact reverse.
And being dyslexic
Is not a curse.

I've tried to explain
Just what I see,
But it's hard
When there's no consistency.

I'll start off great
And read just fine.
Then suddenly
Start skipping lines.

I get frustrated.
I try to hurry.
It makes it worse;
My words get blurry.

My eyes are fine.
I see perfectly clear.
I don't need glasses
For far or near.

I'm not stupid.
I can understand.
But signals get lost
On the way to my hand.

It's not just reading
That's hard for me.
Math nor writing
Come easily.

Being hands-on
Works great for me
Since I see the world
So differently.

I see patterns
And make connections.
I'm a visual thinker
With high expectations.

I know I'll be great.
I've looked back in time.
I belong to a group
With Picasso and Einstein.

A Rise through Guided Failure

I am a failure.
You'll never convince me
I will succeed.
Nothing comes easy, but
I'm lazy, and I don't try.
I refuse to tell myself
That I will be unstoppable because
I have convinced myself
That I am just an idiot.
Say what you want, but I'll never believe
I'll achieve my goals.
Regardless,
I'll never amount to anything,
And I have no reason to believe
That I'm actually very smart.
I struggle in class, and I sit and think,
Is my future really this bleak?

(Now read up.)

My Keeper

My biggest fear
Would have to be
Screwing up so bad
You'd give up on me.

Giving up
I could take.
I'd walk away.
I made the mistake.

What I couldn't take,
Or even conceive,
You listening to others
And starting to believe.

Once you believe,
I'd be willing to bet
It wouldn't take long,
And you'd start to regret.

And if you could do that, too,
It says to me you never knew
How much you meant to me,
How much I appreciated you.

Anyone else, I wouldn't care.
I'm sure I'd be just fine.
I never wanted for you
To think I was a waste of time.

2015.04.18 17:17

A Guiding Light

It's about time.
Someone can finally see
Why school
Has been a struggle for me.

Now it's been noticed,
My weaknesses addressed.
It's becoming easier
For me to do my best.

I really hate
These books I read.
It's so embarrassing,
But it's what I need.

I still compensate,
But it's different now.
My strengths aid my weaknesses,
And I'm learning exactly how.

My whole life
Is starting to change.
I'm letting go
Of this frustration and rage.

I'm interested
In ball once again
And hanging out
With all my old friends.

I want to do good.
I want to succeed.
And thanks to you,
I'm getting the help I need.

I have a reason now.
My goals I will achieve.
In myself, because of you,
I can finally believe.

Sexual Assault

I am a prisoner inside myself. For how long, it's up to me, but until I learn to forgive myself, a prisoner I will be.

A Pedophile's Deception

What do you mean, it was an accident?
Nothing about that even makes sense.
There was nothing even there; what did you trip on … the air?
And with everything around to grab, why did you choose … there?

If it really was an accident, why do I feel this way?
And if nothing really happened, what do I even say?
I tried to tell, but what's the point; I don't have a voice.
You proved that to me the minute you said, "You don't have a choice."

I know the difference between wrong and right,
But this is confusing; I have no insight.
I hate what you're doing, yet it feels good.
I care about you but don't feel that I should.

Because of the good, I deal with the bad.
It's killing me inside, and I just feel sad.
You tell me I'm special and that you're my friend,
But you're giving me nightmares that never end.

Is anyone ever nice just because?
Will everyone manipulate me the way he does?
How will I ever learn who to trust when all I see
Are lies … deception … and … deceit?

Awake in the Night

In the middle of the night,
Seven nights a week,
Lies a young girl
Unable to sleep.

With visions of monsters
Racing in her head,
Awake and on guard,
She sits there in bed.

Thinking and processing,
Confused by what she knows.
Hoping and praying
This isn't how life goes.

But his threats are so real
She knows they are true.
Believing in his lies,
Wondering what to do.

Not knowing who to trust,
Or who she can tell,
She keeps her secret
And remains in hell.

Lost and Confused

Racing heart, butterflies—
What is this that I feel?
Believing in your lies,
Doubting my pain is real.

What you're doing is wrong.
Or at least I think so.
I'm trying to remain strong,
Confused by what I know.

Are you really my friend?
I'm so lost and confused.
From fun that never ends
To feeling so abused.

I know it's "our secret."
Don't understand why
I promised you I'd keep it,
But it just makes me cry.

What you are doing hurts me.
It's changing who I am.
My future I can't see.
Why can't you understand?

Secret Scars

I feel so empty deep inside.
What is it that you've done?
I feel my life is over,
And yet it's barely begun.

Something inside me
Doesn't feel right.
My knees are shaking,
My stomach tight.

My interests are fading.
My future seems bleak.
I'm dying inside
With these secrets I keep.

My insides are burning;
I can't escape this hell.
Inside my head is churning,
Confused by lies you tell.

What you are doing is killing me.
This pain inside is real.
How much more can I take?
My heart's not made of steel.

So when my pain starts building up,
My heart so full of grief,
I grab a knife and cut myself
Just to feel relief.

This person inside me
Is starting to change
From smiles and fun
To anger and rage.

What did I do
To deserve this hell?
And why won't you listen
When I try to tell?

So with no one to tell
Because I can't trust,
Keeping my secrets
Becomes a must!

Stolen Innocence

I just woke up
In a started fright.
How can this happen
In the middle of the night?

I was robbed.
Someone invaded my place,
Leaving me with
This dark, empty space.

I look around.
My whole life is gone.
What do I do?
How can I move on?

First …

I need to get a new lock
So no one can get in.

Then …

I'll stand on guard at night,
Determined it won't happen again.

I won't be needing
A TV;
These visions in my head
Are enough, you see.

I won't be buying
A couch or tables at the end.
No one comes over.
I can't do this to my friends.

Sure, it would be nice
To just call the police.
Maybe then
I can feel some relief.

But …

What he stole
Can't be replaced.
And what he left
Is hard to erase.

And …

This isn't
That type of crime.
It didn't just happen
This one time.

It wasn't material
That was stolen from me.
It was my innocence,
Can't you see?

Night Creeper

The door opens.
Softly you creep
To the bed where
I lay sound asleep.

When you're done
And I finally wake,
I'm left here wondering
What did he take?

I wake in the morning,
Still tired and sore,
Please make it stop.
I can't take anymore.

I know it's my fault.
You warned me, it's true.
If I fell asleep,
What you would do?

You come in my sleep.
You're there when I'm awake.
You follow me to work.
I have no escape

Inside I'm just angry
And so frustrated.
No way to release,
And I just hate it.

I'll hit and kick,
Scream and balk,
From David Banner
To the Incredible Hulk.

This isn't who I am
Or who I want to be.
My pain comes from his joy.
Why can't anyone see?

A Lost Little Girl

She went to the police
And filed a report
About a missing girl.

The description she gave:
"We're about the same age
And both have hair with curls.

I saw her last just yesterday,
Out in the yard
Where she loved to play.

She had a big smile.
She was happy and carefree,
Just like every child should be.

But now she is lost.
She is scared
And all alone.

Please, you have to help me.
Shine your light.
Show her the way home.

I know she will talk.
Please
Just give her a little time
Cuz what she has
To say to you
Will surely blow your mind.

What he did to her
Killed her
Deep inside.

And the little girl
She used to be,
Suddenly up and died.

She used to love
To laugh and play,
But suddenly that changed.

Now she just
Sits around, pissed off
And full of rage.

The young girl who went missing
Is lost deep
Inside of me.

Please tell me
You can find her
And finally set her free."

The Wrong Kid

Summertime, playing ball with a friend.
Now it's time for my fun to end.
"I don't want to go," I repeatedly say.
Why won't you listen? Just let me play.

I can't believe you're making me go.
Why can't you see these signs I throw?
My friend knows something; he called him a creep.
I don't want him to know these secrets I keep.

I walk down the street, nice and slow,
Dreading what's next cuz I already know.
Your threats seem real; your lies seem true.
I'm just a kid, what else can I do?

I hit, scream, put up a fight
Until he grabs that gun on my right.
I don't want to die, not this way.
So I give in, I'm ashamed to say.

Wait, I hear footsteps coming this way.
This weight on my chest is going away.
The door opens; I thought I was finally free.
My heart sank as she walked away from me.

I was so angry, so confused.
I felt dirty, guilty, and used.
I'm done living this hell.
But I'm alone, with no one to tell.

This nightmare has got to end.
You lied to me; you're not my friend.
You made me do things I didn't want to.
You were the adult, I trusted you.

I'm not doing this for you or even for me.
I'm doing it for the other kids I see.
The ones who are happy, not full of fears,
Who sleep through the night, not wake up in tears.

Now you're in jail cuz of the charges I filed.
Never again will you hurt a child.
Forty-two years, I hope you live long.
Think of me and what you did wrong.

I know there were others in the past,
But I'm proud to say I was your last.
Why you chose me I will never know.
Clearly, it was the wrong way to go.

Rooming with Monsters

I'm not afraid of monsters
In my closet or under my bed.
The monsters that scare me
Are living in my head.

The first one showed up,
Scared and all alone.
Then gradually, more move in.
Now they, too, call it home.

It's getting so crowded
There's no room to move.
But how do I evict
When no one will approve.

So I try to be
A triage nurse,
Putting them in order
From bad to worse.

Slowly I start
Kicking them out.
Once there's no more
To talk about.

Some will listen
And just stay gone.
Others come back.
They can't move on.

Now you're worried
What's in my head.
Where were you when
That monster crawled in my bed?

Misunderstanding Why

Why do we question
What we know is wrong?
And why do we feel
It's us who don't belong?

Why do we "choose"
To be abused
When it makes us feel
Dirty, guilty, and used?

Why don't we tell
These secrets we keep,
When these monsters
Won't let us sleep?

I'll tell you why.
If you want to know,
Hang on tight
Cuz here we go.

Sex offenders are good
At what they do.
After all,
They fooled you too.

I did make a choice,
A choice to survive.
I went through hell,
But I'm still alive.

How can I tell
When you push me away,
Tell me I'm a kid,
And that I have no say.

How can I tell
And make you believe?
You won't listen.
You tell me to leave.

You tell me to talk,
I need to be strong.
You think I am weak,
But you are so wrong.

I'm standing here,
Trying to speak.
How the *hell*
Does that make me weak?

You're so worried
What my story will do.
Not to me, of course,
But to you.
You can't stay quiet
And keep the peace.
What's going on
Has got to cease!

So don't ask why.
Don't think we're weak.
Maybe ask yourself
Why you don't want us to speak?

Moving On

I know this world's a much better place
Now that you are gone.
But once again, I'm left here,
Just trying to move on.

"You should be happy; you have closure,"
I hear people say.
But what they hell is closure,
Some magical, "It's OK?"

I know all about psychology
And what statistics say.
Knowing and understanding
Won't take this pain away.

Thoughts in my head, feelings in my heart
Are far from the same.
Still carrying all this guilt,
Knowing I'm not to blame.

Everything, what you said, what I know
Race through my mind.
Thinking of terrible things,
Remembering the kind.

Years, ups and downs; I need to forgive
Shame, guilt, anger, fear.
I need to heal, need to talk.
How, who would want to hear?

I forgive you for all you've done,
The hell you put me through.
Please know this, this act of grace
Is all for me, not you!

Breaking Free

I have a secret
I need to tell
About a time
I lived through hell.

I need to understand
These feelings I feel,
So I can move on
And I can heal.

This is my story.
It is my truth.
So please sit there
And have some couth.

You were not there.
It didn't happen to you,
So don't tell me
What you would do.

Don't ask me why
I went back.
A question I have
For an answer I lack.

Don't ask if I said no
Or put up a fight.
I did what I did;
There's no wrong or right.

You can't understand
What it's like
Fighting daily
For your life.

Sit and listen.
Don't judge or blame.
I'm a survivor,
I have *no shame!*

Finding Fault

Would you blame your car
For getting a dent,
Or blame your house
For not paying the rent?

Would you blame your phone
For getting lost,
Or blame the gas
For raising the cost?

Would you blame the tree
That fell on your house,
Or blame the bread
For attracting a mouse?

You wouldn't do this.
You can clearly see
This way of thinking
Is pure stupidity.

Then why blame a victim
For their assault,
When it's so obvious
It's not their fault?

Victim Talk

First …

When speaking to a victim
Of sexual assault,
Nothing they did
Makes this their fault.

So …

Don't ask what they did
Or tell them what you would do
When you have no idea
The hell they just lived through.

Don't tell them
To "Get over it,"
When you don't have
Nightmares that just won't quit.

Don't tell them it's too hard
To just sit there and hear
When their trying to tell their story
While fighting back their tears.

Don't ask what they were wearing.
It's irrelevant anyway.
Just sit and listen
To what they have to say.

Don't judge.
Don't blame.
They're dealing with
Enough shame.

Because ...

When a victim gets the courage
To finally tell what happened to them,
Your reactions can shut them down,
Ensuring they won't try again.

But ...

We need to speak
So we can heal.
Holding it in
Is no way to deal.

It's Time

Because of you,
I've built this wall,
Letting no one in.
No one at all.

I cannot trust.
Myself, I doubt,
Terrified
My secrets *will g*et out.

Brick by brick,
This wall will grow.
The person inside
No one will know.

The things I enjoy or
Like to do
I've kept secret
Because of you.

Now it's time,
Time to heal.
Time to rid myself
Of this anger I feel.

Now it's time,
Time to try.
Time to deal with all
The trauma in my life.

Listen

You want to know
Why we don't tell
And why we keep
Our secrets, oh, so well?

I'll tell you why.
So sit right there.
First of all,
We're full of fear.

Who do we tell?
Who can we trust?
You don't understand
What this does to us.

They tell us things
And make us believe
That our truths
No one can conceive.

They tell us we're special.
They tell us they care.
It's all so confusing.
Inside we're just scared.

We are much too young;
We can't comprehend.
Is this man bad, or
Is he my friend?

They make us feel guilty.
They make us feel shame.
Tell us we're at fault,
That we will take the blame.

Eventually,
After scrounging around,
A small bit of courage
Is finally found.

So listen up.
Pay close attention.
We may only try once.
Did I forget to mention?

You Were Wrong Too

If I knew then
What I know now,
You'd be in jail.
I just didn't know how.

You knew all along,
Yet nothing was said.
You just closed your eyes
Or quickly turned your head.

To me, your role in this
Was even worse.
Your head is straight,
But his mind is cursed.

He has issues
And no control.
You're just weak
And ignored it all.

He was wrong
And should have to pay.
But so should you,
I would have to say.

How could you sit there,
Being of no use,
While a child becomes a victim
Of your husband's abuse.

My Story

Don't tell me that I'm beautiful.
He told me that before,
As he led me to his room
And slowly closed the door.

Don't tell me that I'm special.
I was "special" to him too.
We had secret games we played
That no one ever knew.

Don't tell me that I'm pretty.
I know it isn't true.
Inside I just feel dirty
Because of the things he made me do.

Don't tell me that I'm strong
When all I feel is weak.
I can't even find the strength
To open my mouth and speak.

Don't tell me that I'm tough
When I obviously lost the fight
And too ashamed to tell someone.
So I cry in bed each night.

So when I find the courage,
The best thing you can do,
Just sit there and listen
To the things I say to you.

I'm not telling you my story
So that you can relate.
I'm telling you my story
So my truth I can validate.

I'm telling you my story
So I can finally heal.
I need to face my trauma.
Stop pretending it's no big deal.

I'm telling you my story
To finally put it to use.
So I can now help others
To cope with their abuse.

The Light within a Pedophile's Storm

Without warning,
Without alarm,
This storm touched down,
Leaving destruction, causing harm.

I look in the distance.
I look for an escape.
Dark clouds roll in;
I disassociate.

And as the rain
Pours from the skies,
Tears of pain
Fall from my eyes.

The winds are getting stronger.
I don't know what to do.
I have all my windows boarded,
So no one can get through.

Then lightning strikes
And admits a glow.
It shows me my strengths
Buried deep below.

I weathered the storm
And became the light.

Illuminating darkness,
I was ready to fight.

I conquered the storm
And have no shame.
I know my strength
Comes from my pain.

A Survivor's Story

I was a victim
Of sexual abuse.
Don't blame me;
There is no use.

Internalizing blame
Is what I do.
I'm just a kid,
Not an adult, like you.

I will keep my secrets
Locked up tight,
And cry myself
To sleep each night.

My grades will drop.
My behavior will change.
There will be ups and downs
And fits of rage.

But I'll stay silent,
Not letting it out.
My head confused,
My heart full of doubt.

And as I grow,
So will my pain.
And then comes along
Guilt and shame.

But if I continue
To keep it in,
It will destroy me
From within.

Only I
Can stop this pain.
I realize now
I'm not to blame.

I'm ready to talk,
To scream, to shout.
It's time
I let these secrets out.

Doing it my way
And at my own pace,
This is my journey;
It's not a race.

I'm in control.
I'm the driver.
Once a victim,
Now a *survivor!*

PTSD and Miscellaneous Emotions

Keep telling yourself you're nothing, and nothing is what you'll be;
tell yourself you're something, and something is what you'll see.

The Tour

Come, please, step inside.
Let me take you for a ride.
Sit back, hold on tight,
Learn something new, you just might.

Everything, first, last
Were left here from traumas past.
Look left and then look right.
It will give you much insight.

First is lost and found.
Please take a good look around.
These things come and go.
Memories of things, you know.

Next we'll go here.
We call this the room of fear.
Flashbacks and nightmares
Fill the air; come—if you dare.

Then, we have "the cage,"
Filled with anger, guilt, and rage.
Come here, let it out.
Hit, kick, even scream and shout.

Or come here and stay
If you just need to get away.
It's a great escape.
Disassociate.

Here we end our tour.
Anytime, come back, learn more.
Maybe now you'll see
What it's like, PTSD.

If Anyone Cares

This smile on my face
Is no longer real.
It's really dark inside this place,
And pain is all I feel.

This place is empty,
Not one person found.
I am lost, hurt, broken, angry.
But no one is around.

No one understands
The hell I lived through.
Their judgment, blame, I can't withstand.
So shut down, I will do.

My secrets, I keep
Locked up deep inside.
Can't eat, sleep, and refuse to speak.
Just want to run and hide.

As I lie in bed,
Scared and all alone,
I drift away inside my head.
It's safe and far from home.

Each night as I sleep,
Flashbacks and nightmares
Fill my head; visions softly creep.
Alone, scared, distant stares.

Morning I will wake
Ready, and drying tears.
But this smile, you see, it's still fake.
If anyone cares.

Misdirected Apologies

I'm sorry ...

... I have no voice.
... No one will listen.
... My signs get ignored.
... No one notices.
... I can't talk.
... No one believes me.
... I believed him.
... He lied to me.
... I trusted him.
... He manipulated me.
... I'm confused.
... It felt good.
... I feel gross.
... I feel shame.
... I feel guilt.
... I allowed it to go on.
... I went back.
... No one questioned.
... No one cares.
... No one understands.
... I'm not strong enough.

... I have no rights.
... I am a victim.
... I am a child.

K. A. R.

Can't eat, terrified to sleep.
No one cares or asks why.
Grades drop, trouble all the time,
No one listens, hears my cry.

Why can't you see this isn't me?
I'm broken, lost, confused,
Screaming, wanting to be heard.
Ignored, still being abused.

Potential, it's not in me.
Everything I do, I fail.
Everyone's given up; they
Believe I belong in jail.

I know there is good in me.
I have goals, hopes, dreams too.
When everyone's against you,
What are you supposed to do?

All I need is just one, one
Person to take a chance on me.
Someone to see what I see.
Someone to believe in me.

For me, that person is you,
Though I don't understand why.
I am nothing to you.
Why bother, why even try?

I can't thank you enough.
Things you did, things you would say
Have definitely made me
The person I am today.

The Me No One Can See

No one knows
The real me.
They only know
What I allow them to see.

Childhood trauma
Has made me this way,
Never knowing the "right" thing
To do or say.

I get so lonely
And depressed.
Inside my head
Is such a mess.

I'll refuse to talk;
There's too much shame.
Cuz when I do,
It's me they blame.

"Forget about it,"
Is what they say.
How, when
Flashbacks fill my day?

Then each night
The nightmares appear.
Startled awake,
Sweating in fear.

I'll get so angry
I'll just shake,
Looking around
For something to break.

I'll hurt myself.
I'll scream, I'll shout,
Just trying
To get these feelings out.

No one knows
The real me.
Thanks so much,
PTSD!

Never Enough

Trying to please you
Is getting tough.
Nothing I do
Is ever enough.

I never know
What to do or say.
Your reactions change
Depending on the day.

If all is perfect, and
I do just what you say,
Then I'm guaranteed
To have a perfect day.

If I do something
You don't like,
Instantly
It becomes a fight.

You fill my head
With guilt and shame.
It's not my fault.
We're not the same.

I know you want me
To be like you.
And parts of me
Wants that too.

There's more to me
Than you know,
But I'm ashamed
To let it show.

You taught me that,
Can't you see,
By making me hide
My identity.

I just don't get it.
I don't understand.
You seem so ashamed
Of who I am.

Pain Reliever

I hate it here
So, so bad.
I'm never happy.
Just always mad

I hate these secrets
I have to hide.
They're tearing me up
Deep inside.

I hate this person
I've become.
At seventeen,
I'm still so young.

I can't talk.
I've got no one to tell.
So I push it down
And fight like hell.

I can't do this
On my own.
I feel so lost,
So alone.

This pain inside
Starts building up.
So I grab a knife
And start to cut.

The physical pain
Is nothing you see.
It doesn't compare
To what's inside of me.

I'm not trying to die.
That's not my belief.
What else can I do?
I need some relief.

Dreaming

I used to lie in bed
Thinking of what I might be
When I became an adult,
And people could see me.

I wanted to know sign language.
It was such a fascination.
At only six years old, I didn't know
It could even be a career destination.

I thought about being
A cop or maybe a firefighter.
Imagining helping others
Just made my future seem brighter.

I thought I'd make a great lawyer;
I love a good debate.
But when reality set in,
This, too, I must abate.

I wanted to be a teacher,
Help kids just like me.
But how many teachers do you know
With a learning disability?

The one thing that never changed—
And I thought about so often—
All I ever really wanted
Was not to be *forgotten*.

Forgotten

I'm all alone.
I'm lost and scared.
No one looks for me;
No one cares.

I'll just sit here
With a tear in my eye,
Wonder if you'll miss me
If tomorrow I die.

Will you even notice
I'm no longer there?
Will it even matter?
Will you even care?

Please don't forget me
Or blame me for this too.
I've tried so hard
To be like you.

Think of the good,
If you can.
Help others to see
Just who I am.

Not everything
I've done was wrong,
So don't resent me
When I'm gone.

I put up a front,
And I may look "tough,"
But inside I know
I'm just never enough.

Help me to leave
Something behind,
A good piece of me
To stay on their mind.

And once I'm gone,
Maybe then you will see
There was actually
Some good in me.

A PTSD Wonderland

Just like Alice,
I fell into a well,
Surrounded by secrets
With no one to tell.

I didn't get here
By drinking a potion.
But my head is spinning;
There's too much commotion.

It's dark in here,
And I'm all alone.
I feel so lost.
I may never get home.

Fortunately
I'm not into cats,
So for me, at least,
There's none of that.

My friend Mr. Rabbit
Is always late.
And I, of course,
Love to disassociate.

The Queen of Hearts
Is a narcissist.
Talking to her,
I feel so dismissed.

I get so angry.
It's like I don't matter.
You can call me
The Mad Hatter.

And when I feel
I just need a chiller,
I toke it up
Like a caterpillar.

This isn't just
A dream for me.
This is my life
With PTSD!

2018.03.07 18:50

Help!

I'm in the deep
Water; I'm treading.
I know I need help.
It's the asking I'm dreading.

A boat comes by
And offers to help.
It's not what I want.
I can do it myself.

So they pass by.
I continue to tread.
They're weighing me down,
These secrets in my head.

Another boat
Comes by to help.
Once again
I'll do it myself.

I'll figure it out
On my own.
I don't need you,
So leave me alone.

I can't keep treading.
I'm going to die.
I have to accept help
From the next boat to pass by.

It's time I swallow my pride,
Let go of this shame.
This wasn't my fault.
I'm not the one to blame!

Changing History

Many times
I've been asked
If I could,
Would I go back?

Would I change
What's happened to me?
Do I wish my past
Was more a fantasy?

I've thought long and hard
About all that I have seen,
And I can honestly say
I wouldn't change a thing.

That's not to say
I'd do it again.
I wouldn't wish that
On my worst friend.

But I wouldn't go back
And change it, you see.
Because if I did,
I wouldn't be me.

I hate what happened.
Don't get me wrong.
But my struggles, my fight,
Are what make me strong.

A Toy Box of Emotions

Like a clown,
I'll put on a show.
I'll fake a smile,
Then off I go.

Like a yo-yo,
I'm spinning around.
You pull me up,
Then push me down.

Like a doll,
I don't say a thing.
Sitting quietly
Until you pull my string.

Like G. I. Joe,
I'm ready to fight,
Combating nightmares
That appear each night.

But …

Unlike a unicorn,
I can't fly away.
So in my head
Is where I stay.

And …

Unlike Superman,
I'm not made of steel.
This pain inside of me
Is actually very real.

This box is getting cluttered.
There are blocks scattered about.
I think it's finally time
To start throwing these toys out!

Trash Day

Forgiving is not forgetting,
No matter what people say.
And in no way are you saying
That what happened is now okay.

Forgiveness is not meant for them,
And I think it's just too kind.
But if I don't do something soon,
I'm going to lose my mind.

I still don't know how to forgive.
It's such an act of grace.
But I'm trying something new
So this frown I can replace.

I can't call it "forgiveness";
It just creeps me out.
It seems more fitting to say,
"I'm taking the garbage out."

Bags of anger and hatred
Are piling at my door.
He left so much garbage here
I can barely see the floor

So one by one
I'm starting to pitch
These bags that make me
Such a bitch.

And little by little
I start to see
Just how positive
This is for me.

I'm letting go
And moving on
And finally loving
This journey I'm on.

Looking Back

I wasn't born to be a narcissist,
So why is it I feel like this?
That's the beauty of hindsight, don't you know,
Looking back, learning, so you can grow.

Now I think I may understand.
Come with me; take my hand.
Let's look back, so we can see
Exactly how things came to be.

From day 1 I didn't trust.
You took offense; I could never adjust.
As I grew up, we grew apart.
It's not your fault; we were doomed from the start.

The lessons I learned from the things you said
Never go away; they're always in my head.
I understand that was not your intent,
And I misunderstood the message you sent.

No matter how clear my memory,
The truth was always kept from me.
I had no privacy, my room not my own,
My opinion didn't matter, I was not grown.

You put me down to make me tough,
But what I learned was I'm never enough.
You tell me to leave, you can't look at me.
Why can't you love me unconditionally?

I can't continue to dismiss
What's in my head, I need to fix.
I can't keep going, not like this.
You've turned me into a narcissist.

Now I'm grown, and I am strong.
But in this place I don't belong.
I'm looking back and letting go.
Once again my smile will show.

This is not who I am or
Who I was meant to be.
I'm dealing with my trauma
So I can finally be *me*.

Healing

I am not my trauma.
I am not a victim.
But when I tell my truth,
I just hear criticism.

What were you wearing?
What did you do
To make him do
Those things to you?

Did you say no?
Did you put up a fight?
Why not tell someone
That's just not right?

It's over now.
Just move along.
You know what they say,
"Trauma makes you strong."

No
It doesn't!

Trauma is trauma.
Just like it sounds,
It tears you up,
It knocks you down.

Your thinking gets distorted.
It's hard to clearly see,

And this thinking, though untrue,
Becomes your reality.

With visions spinning
In your head,
Your pillow wet,
Your eyes red,

You lie there thinking
Only the worst,
Wondering why
Your life's so cursed.

But ...

If you just get up
And start to move,
Slowly you will see
Your life start to improve.

Tell yourself
That you can
Set a goal,
Make a plan.

Talk to someone,
Get it out,
Empty your head
Of the guilt and doubt.

Allow yourself
To release the pain.
Start redirecting
All the blame.

Trauma may have brought me here,
But it's not where I belong.
And it wasn't the trauma, but the fight and the struggle
That has really made me strong.

Undefined

"What am I?" you ask,
Like what nationality.
I have no idea.
I'm an adoptee.

"Really, you were adopted?
That's so cool," people say.
Or I get the look of pity
And, "I'm sorry you were thrown away."

I have a good life.
My parents love me.
But I have so many questions
About my identity.

When I go to school,
It's so chaotic.
I'm not just adopted,
I'm also dyslexic.

Then more questions
Come my way.
I still have no answers,
So I have nothing to say.

I've asked these questions
Myself, you see.
I'm just so curious.
Who will I be?

Now one more thing
That's not my fault—
Adoption, dyslexia,
Now sexual assault.

Don't ask me questions.
Don't try to blame.
I've had enough
Of this damn game.

I was adopted, but I'm not an adoptee.
I am dyslexic and have a learning disability.
I was assaulted but not a victim, you see.
Childhood trauma does *not* define me!

Printed in the United States
by Baker & Taylor Publisher Services